HOW TO FIND
PEACE WITH GOD

SETTING YOU FREE

"When life is heavy and hard to take, go off by yourself.
Enter the silence. Bow in prayer. Don't ask questions:
Wait for hope to appear. Don't run from trouble.
Take it full-face. The "worst" is never the worst."
- Lamentations 3:28-30 The Message

DEREK WHITE

Library of Congress Catalog Number:
1-2449432191

Printed in the USA

Front and Back Cover designed by
Darrell Andrews Jr.

Copyright 2015

ISBN 978-0-9964894-0-9

DEDICATION

I'd like to dedicate this book to my mother
Kathleen Sheryll White,
who is a devout Christian, continues to do
God's work in the world, and has done a LOT for me
for as long as I've been alive.
May I continue to strive to be as great of
a person as she is.

TABLE OF CONTENTS

Prologue

I was born in Miami, Florida on April 2, 1988. It wasn't until the age of four when I was diagnosed with Asperger Syndrome, which is a form of autism. Fast-forwarding to the age of fourteen; my freshman year in high school. I was beginning to get a better understanding of what Asperger Syndrome is and the effect it had on my personal struggles and my being different from others. Fortunately, I grew up in the church, and I was influenced by my mother to focus on God's plan for my life, in spite of having Asperger's.

The point I'm making is that you do not have to let an obstacle prevent you from succeeding in anything you do. You can either use it as an excuse or you can learn to cope with it and use it as a stepping stone. In my years of living with Asperger's, I began to look at it as a disability. I even thought of it as a curse. But, because it's a part of my life I chose to cope with its negative and positive effects. I'm choosing to use it as a stepping stone to walk in what God has for me and how He sees me. I've learned to look at the "big picture," which is my purpose. God gave each of us a purpose.

I believe that one of my purposes is to write this book, helping you and I find peace with God, regardless of the challenges we may experience.

Derek White

Introduction

Some people are unaware that everyone suffers at some point in their lives. We all struggle with different things, whether it's financially, our health, love lives, family issues, etc. We all get stressed and depressed here and there. But do we have to wallow in it? NO! We definitely do not. My mother once told me "At the end of every struggle is a *blessing*." She's a wise lady. Her saying goes along with these other sayings, "Everything happens for a reason", "Things will get worse before they get better," and "Every cloud has a silver lining."

How did my mother come up with her saying? I think it comes from her studying the Bible for many years. That's the greatest part of living our lives. We have the Word of God to guide us and protect us from harm's way. I mean let's be honest. Life can get very difficult in every way, shape, and form, which often puts us in distress. But if we take at least a few minutes each day to read our Bibles, I guarantee some of that weight will be taken off our shoulders.

I'm going to go over several scriptures from God's Word that might help guide you and set you free from any kind of distress. Life is too short to be unhappy, so just breeze through it with a smile and put all your troubles in God's hands, and in the end you will be rewarded. The purpose of this book is to help make your life easier. I hope you can find peace and comfort as you read this book. God bless you.

CHAPTER ONE

SETTLING

My initial motivation for writing this book was for self-healing. I ended a rough relationship, that's been on-and-off for two years. It was a painful experience for me. I was dating a young lady, who I met thru her mother. I used to work with her mother at a home improvement store. The mother thought so highly of me that she wanted me to meet her daughter. So I met her daughter, and we liked each other *at first*, which lead us to dating. *At first*, I was happy and had the idea that I've found Ms. Right. Her mother would even call me her son-in-law often, but as time went by I realized that we were not right for one another because we had a hard time getting along.

Why did I let the relationship go on for two years? I had the impression that this young lady was my only option; that it was either her or no one. I found her to be very attractive and her mother would always brag about how many other guys would love to be with her. I had the impression that if we broke up, I would be much more unhappy, so I *settled*. That is until I had the courage to break it off with her, and realize that it is better to be single and happy than it is to be in a relationship and miserable.

It was this relationship that lead me to writing this book, because even though I ended this chapter of my life, I was still a little heartbroken, so I made the choice to seek God and develop a better relationship with Him. I started by praying and reading His word.

CHAPTER TWO

FINANCIAL STRUGGLES

Now, although I found peace with God, I still encountered another challenge on a completely different level. A few months after my ex and I broke up for good, I lost my job at the home improvement store, after working there for four years.

Financially, things were beginning to get rough for me at that point. Fortunately, I found a job at a discount store shortly afterwards to hold me over for a while. The problem was I wasn't making as much money at the discount store as I was at the home improvement store. I was *struggling*. Employees at discount stores are usually people who live at home with their parents, such as high school students or individuals who just want a part-time job to make some extra money. But there I was, a grown man in his 20s, working a minimum wage job.

What am I going to do? Am I going to get evicted

from my apartment? What's going to happen to me? God, do you hear me? How will I survive? All these questions, concerns, and all this worrying was bombarding my mind. I was determined to make sure I was going to get out of this mess! I spent some time looking for a second job or a much better paying job. My disadvantage at first was that I never finished college, which explains why the discount store was the only job I could find so quickly after I was terminated from the home improvement store.

I did not lose hope though. I was very confident that God would help me, because He knew I needed a way out of this financial struggle. Fortunately, a co-worker and friend of mine who also worked at the discount store with me, informed me that he was in the process of being hired by a very large financial institution. He also informed me that this financial institution was always hiring. So, I submitted my application online, and I repeatedly prayed for God to help me get this job.

A couple of days later, I received a phone call from

a very nice lady, who happened to be a recruiter for the financial institution. I told her a little about myself and she scheduled me for an interview! Words could not describe my excitement, because I saw it as a door that God was opening for me. I arrived about a half an hour early in a suit for my interview to make a good impression. I was being interviewed by two different managers. I went above and beyond to make sure I impressed them, by being filled with positive energy and making eye contact with them the entire time.

When I left the building, I felt very good about the interview. I was confident that I was going to get the job. And I did!!! I give all the credit to *that man upstairs*. The reason I was terminated from the home improvement store, which lead to my struggling at the discount store, was because this is where God wants me to be as of now. God will always have a purpose for your pain, a reason for your struggles, and *a reward for your faithfulness!* If God wants me to remain an employee at this financial institution, this may even become a career for me. Praise Him!

CHAPTER THREE

ASPERGER SYNDROME/AUTISM

What is Asperger Syndrome?

As I mentioned in the prologue, Asperger Syndrome is an autism spectrum disorder (ASD). The autism spectrum describes multiple conditions ranging from social impairment, communication difficulties, repetitive behaviors and interests, sensory issues, lack of eye contact, and in some cases, obsession with specific, often unusual topics. Children can be diagnosed with these symptoms as early as eighteen months or even younger in some cases. Males are four times more likely to have ASD than females.

Asperger Syndrome is considered to be on the "high functioning" end of the autistic spectrum. Compared to those affected by other forms of ASD, those with Asperger Syndrome do not have difficulties in language development. Some are shown to be articulate, often in a specified field of interest, such as math, science, or music. While an individual's symptoms can range from mild to severe, their IQs are typically in the normal to very superior range.

How is Asperger Syndrome diagnosed?

Asperger Syndrome is often diagnosed when a child or adult begins to have serious difficulties in school, the workplace, or their personal lives. Indeed, many adults with Asperger's receive their diagnosis when seeking help for related issues such as anxiety or depression. Diagnosis tends to center primarily on difficulties with social interactions.

My experience with Asperger Syndrome

Growing up with Asperger's in a single parent home was never easy for myself or my mother. I had my fair share of struggling in school, low self-esteem, depression, trouble making friends, etc. It was almost everyday that I would feel lost with no sense of direction.

My mother definitely had a challenge in raising a

child like me. She often had to work two or three jobs to take care of me in addition to putting a lot of energy into making sure I got through school.

Things got so difficult and so extreme, I was placed in special education and my mother had taken me to see several psychiatrists over the years. With us living in such a cruel world, I would get teased, made fun of, and ridiculed for being different.

But then, I came to realize that there is absolutely nothing wrong with being different! That's what makes us each unique. The world would be one big boring place if God made us all the same. He created us to be different because we each have a different purpose. This is what we are called to do; to seek and fulfill God's purpose for our lives.

Although, I still cope with the effects of Asperger Syndrome to this day, I eventually made a choice to seek God's plan for my life. With a lot of counseling, finding a church that feeds my spirit, and reading the Bible, it wasn't as difficult as you might imagine for me to become a student of the Lord. It wasn't as difficult because I had to make that choice. I wanted better for myself. Always remember that no matter what you may struggle with, God loves you, and wants to have a relationship with you. Your value does not decrease based on someone's inability to see your worth. If you didn't have a purpose, you would not be here.

"Don't copy the behavior and customs of this world, but let God transform you into a new person by changing the way you think. Then you will learn to know God's will for you, which is good and pleasing and perfect" (Romans 12:2).

CHAPTER FOUR

MY MOTHER & FATHER/RELATIONSHIPS

Now let's get back to my relationship issue. At this point in my lifetime, I've come to realize that the reason I stayed in a dysfunctional relationship with my ex, and settled for less than what I knew I deserved could primarily be because I didn't have my father in my life. I didn't have a male role model around to teach me what a man should expect from a woman. I was raised by my mother. My older sister, Avrielle had been around to look out for me as well, but I only had one parent, and I was growing up around women only.

My father was not a good provider for my mother, my sister, and I when my parents were married. We were living in Kansas City, Missouri. My father was a lawyer. He was very well-educated. He took the bar exam in three different states and aced them each time. Academically, he was brilliant, but when it came to working and keeping a job, he was not successful. My dad always had an excuse for not wanting to work.

He was once offered a job that would've paid him a beginning salary of $60k per year. He felt that 60k per year wasn't enough money, so he declined the job. Then my uncle, my mom's brother, referred my dad to a high salary, six-figure position with his company. So my dad flew all the way to Michigan to interview for this position, then when he flew back home, he said to my mother, "That was the ugliest man I've ever seen," talking about the employer. My father *never* wanted to work. My mother was carrying the entire family, including my father, which was too much weight on one person, especially a woman.

My parents ended up getting a divorce. My mother and I moved from Kansas City to Elkton, Maryland, to be closer to our relatives on my mother's side, and because my mother found another job out there. Avrielle had to stay behind with my dad temporarily. She was a senior in high school and was close to graduating, so she wasn't able to transfer her credits to a high school in Maryland.

I grew up living with my mother for many years until I was able to move out on my own. When my sister graduated from high school, she got a scholarship and went off to college in Atlanta, Georgia, and my father went to live with his mother, my grandmother in Chicago, Illinois.

My mother took care of me and supported my sister when she needed it, all by herself, without any help from my father. My mother is also well-educated. She holds two Master's Degrees and a career in Speech Pathology for many years.

Due to my growing up without a father, or a male role model, I learned about life from a female's perspective. One reason my past relationships with women hadn't worked out was because I didn't have a man around to show me how to deal with women from a male's point of view.

My mother taught me how to be a gentleman, and to love God and respect the people around me, but I didn't have a father to teach me how to be a man. Along the way, God has put people in my life that helped me to keep my head on straight, in addition to my mother, such as other relatives, my friends from my church, my pastor, and the list goes on.

Tyrese Gibson described in his book, "How to Get Out of Your Own Way" what a "bottom line" is. He describes it as your own personal boundary that you do not let anyone cross. The purpose of this bottom line is to put a limit on how much negativity you take from other people. Tyrese stresses how important it is to have this because it's a reflection of how you feel about yourself. If you really love yourself, as you should, you won't let anyone cross your bottom line.

If I had this mentality, if I had a father-figure, if I knew about this "bottom line", I would not have continued to stay in that dysfunctional relationship with my ex. But now I know, and I thank God for all that I went through with my ex. I don't have any regrets, and I don't hold anything against her. Instead, I forgave her, and used this as my motivation for writing this book. It was a learning experience and a stepping stone.

Now I'm at the point where I know what I want in a

female. I know what to expect and I know not to settle. I know what my standards are.

CHAPTER FIVE

SUFFERING

"Sometimes we'll look at "disasters" in our lives and think God has abandoned us, but little do you know...
God is setting you up for a major blessing! Don't look at where you are... look at where you're heading!"
~ UNKNOWN

WHY BAD THINGS HAPPEN TO GOOD PEOPLE

Job 1:1 - 2:13

As we read the Book of Job, we discover that Job, the book's main character, lost everything he had, and it wasn't his fault. Job was a good man who lost his children, wealth, and his health. Day by day, he was struggling to understand why this was happening to him. Then, it became clear that he was not meant to know the reasons. But as we read the Book of Job, we find that Job was being tested. Even after Job lost everything, he still kept his faith in God.

Pain can help us grow. These are good words to remember when we face our loss and depression. Because Job did not understand *why* he suffered, his faith in God had a chance to grow.

God does not eliminate all suffering when we follow Him. Also, good behavior is not always rewarded. Rewards for good and punishment for evil are under God's control. They are given out according to His timetable.

We must experience life as Job did, which is to take life one day at a time, and without every answer to all of life's questions. Although we may not always understand the pain we experience, it can draw us closer to God in the end. Like Job, we have a choice: Will we *trust God* no matter what? Or will we falsely believe that God doesn't really care?

Acts 12:2-11

Why did God let James die and miraculously save Peter? Why are some children physically disabled, while others are athletically gifted? Again, we don't have all the answers. Life is full of difficult questions. The reason for this is because we do not see all that God sees. He's too advanced for us. God has chosen to allow evil in this world *temporarily*, but we can still trust Him to guide us, because He has promised to destroy all of evil eventually.

In the meantime, we can count on God to help us *use our suffering* to strengthen us and praise Him. What doesn't kill us only makes us stronger, right? So, why not *use our suffering* and *embrace* it to make us stronger believers? Remember, at the end of every struggle is a blessing, and God is in control.

Romans 8:28-29

Everyday God is working in everything. This does not mean that all that happens to us is good. Whatever you may be going through, God is at work. Evil may be very active in this world, but God is able to turn every bit of it around for a whole lot of good. Keep in mind that God is not working to keep us happy, but to fulfill

27

his purpose.

God's ultimate goal for us is to make us like Jesus (1 John 3:2). We discover our true selves as we become more and more like him. How can we become more like Jesus? (1) By reading and meditating on the Word; (2) By studying his life and teachings throughout the Gospels; (3) By praying;

(4) By being filled with his Spirit; and (5) By doing his work in the world.

EVERYTHING HAPPENS FOR A REASON

Exodus 5:22-23

Moses was getting frustrated with God because he believes that God has not rescued his people from Pharaoh. Moses expected everything to be solved as quickly as he wanted them to be. But what Moses didn't realize is when God is at work, suffering, distress, setbacks, and hardship may still occur.

Problems develop our character and patience by teaching us to (1) be humble; (2) be driven away from worldly pleasures; (3) pray; (4) be more compassionate towards others who are suffering; (5) trust God to do what is best for us; (6) respect and honor God during the situation; (7) remember that God will never abandon us; (8) seek God's plan for us, and (9) remember that God is in control.

You see, it would be easy for us to take the easy way out. Anyone can smoke, drink, or just run away from their problems because it *lacks* discipline. *Anyone* can do these things; but if you follow those nine steps above, it will make you a better person and many blessings will come your way. Smoking, drinking, running away, etc. are behaviors that will *never* be rewarded.

"You can enter God's Kingdom only through the narrow gate. The highway to hell is broad, and it's gate is wide for the many who choose that way. But the gateway to life is very narrow and the road is difficult, and only a few ever find it" (Matthew 7:13-14).

1 Thessalonians 3:1-3

Some think that troubles are always caused to punish us for our sins, or by lacking faith. This may be true in some cases, but trials may be a part of God's plan for believers, regardless of what we've done. Experiencing problems and hardships can build character (James 1:2-4), and sensitivity toward others who may be suffering as well (2 Corinthians 1:3-7). Problems are unavoidable for God's children, but as you put God first and humble yourselves to him, your troubles become a sign of effective Christian living.

Philippians 1:29

Paul considered suffering to be a *privilege* because we could be suffering for Jesus, as he did for us. By nature, we as humans do not consider suffering a privilege. However, when we suffer it could provide a good example for ourselves and others, if we are representing Jesus.

Suffering has these additional benefits: (1) It can take your focus off of earthly treasures; (2) it strengthens the faith of those undergoing it; (3) we can use it as an *opportunity* to live as humble people of God.

Jesus, being the most amazing person who ever lived, suffered for us on that cross. God sent him so that we would not have to suffer for eternity. So why not use our personal suffering to build our character and strengthen our faith. Don't resent it or let it tear you apart, because that sure isn't what Jesus did.

1 Peter is a very good book to read for suffering Christians. Its purpose is to offer encouragement and direction to living holy lives in the midst of suffering. With that being said, I highly recommend reading 1 Peter in addition to this book for extra strength.

CHAPTER SIX

WHAT YOU SAY vs. WHAT GOD SAYS

"If you're trying to achieve, there will be roadblocks. I've had them; everybody has had them. But obstacles don't have to stop you. If you run into a wall, don't turn around and give up. Figure out how to climb it, go through it, or walk around it."
~ MICHAEL JORDAN

YOU SAY	GOD SAYS	SCRIPTURE
I can't figure it out	I will direct your steps	Proverbs 3:5-6
I'm too tired	I will give you rest	Matthew 11:28-30
It's impossible	All things are possible	Luke 18:27
Nobody loves me	I love you	John 3:16
I can't forgive myself	I forgive you	Romans 8:1
It's not worth it	It will be worth it	Romans 8:28
I'm not smart enough	I will give you wisdom	1 Corinthians 1:30
I'm not able	I am able	2 Corinthians 9:8
I can't go on	My grace is sufficient	2 Corinthians 12:9

I can't do it	You can do all things	Philippians 4:13
I can't manage	I will supply all your needs	Philippians 4:19
I'm afraid	I have not given you fear	2 Timothy 1:7
I feel all alone	I will never leave you	Hebrews 13:5
I'm always worried and frustrated	Cast all your cares on ME	1 Peter 5:7

CHAPTER SEVEN

MY FATHER'S PASSING

I hadn't seen my father or anyone on his side of the family since I was twelve years old. However, recently, I received a phone call from my mother when I was at home one night, asking me to come to her house immediately because it was urgent. So, I went to my mother's house as fast as I could, and to my surprise, a cousin of mine from my father's side was there. His name was Bobby. It was shocking, yet nice to see him after nearly twenty years. He told us he was living in Chadds Ford, Pennsylvania, which was only about a half hour from where my mother and I lived. He didn't even know where we were at first. He had to make a few phone calls and search the web to find my mother's address. My mother and I were enjoying his company, and catching up with him for a few minutes....

But then, Bobby told me the reason he was reaching out to us. He told me my father passed away the night before at my grandmother's house. He died of a massive heart attack, however he went out peacefully. My grandmother kept calling him and calling him, but when he wouldn't respond, she touched him, and his hand felt really cold. I could only imagine how my grandmother must've taken this. When I was told this, my eyes started to water, because it was my dad, despite us not having a relationship. That moment showed me how important it is to cherish your loved ones, because tomorrow is never promised. You just never know.

My job gave me two weeks off for bereavement time. My cousin, Bobby and I flew out to Chicago for my dad's funeral. We stayed at my aunt's, Bobby's mother's house for a few days. Bobby took care of all my traveling expenses, which I was very grateful for. My sister didn't come, because my father never paid much attention to her. He favored me, between the two of us because I was a boy, so it would've been too much for her to handle, emotionally, if she came.

While I was out there, I was reunited with many relatives I hadn't seen since I was a child. I met my aunts, uncles, cousins, my grandmother, etc. I grew up with my mother and her side of the family all these years, so words couldn't describe what I was feeling when I was around my father's side of the family all of a sudden. I remembered most of them, including my grandmother, and I remembered her house exactly the way it was, since I was there last as a little boy. It was Deja-vu. There were pictures of my sister and I when we were little, all around the house. That whole experience was tough, but I made it through. I can honestly say I miss my dad a little, even though he wasn't in my life.

The good thing about me coming out to his funeral was that I got to reconnect with my family on his side, which is the other half of where I come from. I am thankful for this in spite of the occasion it took for this to happen. I've gotten to know them and I made the decision to stay in touch with them, because they were very hospitable to me, and they showed me all the love and support they could, even though we haven't been around each other.

CHAPTER EIGHT

COUNT THE BLESSINGS

As God says in Jeremiah 29:11(NLT), "For I know the plans I have for you," says the Lord. "They are plans for good and not for disaster, to give you future and a hope." He has definitely followed through with that scripture in my life. Everything that I am, everything I had gone through, and will go through; I give thanks to God. My character would not be as well-built, if I hadn't endured a few things. After all that I've been through, I can look at where I am now and consider myself blessed. God has blessed me with a mother and a sister as my closest relatives who care for me and keep my best interest at heart, as I do for them. God has blessed me with a job, which pays me what I need to survive, and I'm even able to go back to school for tuition reimbursement, thru this financial institution.

Even though I don't have a degree right now, God helped me get this job, which prefers college graduates, but I got it because of the other gifts He has given me. My pastor once said, "You can have as many degrees as you want, but if you don't know God's word, you don't have a real education." The list can go on about what God has done for me and what God has done for you. I am highly favored and you are highly favored, simply because we were made in God's image.

People who are happy and joyful are this way, not because they have everything they want, but because they are thankful for the things they already have. They appreciate the small things in life. If you have both your parents, if you have a job, a car, a family, your life; give God thanks. Cherish the things you have, because there's always someone who wishes they have the privileges you may be taking for granted.

CHAPTER NINE

LIFE IS TOO SHORT

"I know from personal experience how damaging it can be to live with bitterness and unforgiveness. I like to say it's like taking poison and hoping your enemy will die. And it really is harmful for us to live this way."
~ JOYCE MEYER

WHAT DOES GOD REALLY WANT FROM ME?

Numbers 9:23

The Israelites camped and traveled with God's guidance. When you are guided by God, you know you are where God wants you. Whether you know it or not, there is no better feeling than being where God wants you, so it is very important to always listen for God's instructions.

Direction from God is much more important than direction from anyone else. It's all about *His purpose for your life*. Discover what He wants you to do and where

He wants you to be, simply by asking Him and listening for His answers.

Judges 21:25

During the time of the judges, the people of Israel suffered a lot. Everyone experienced trouble because they did whatever they pleased. They had no relationship with God. This produced horrible results. Our society today is similar in many ways. Many people live according to their own desires, instead of God's.

When people behave selfishly and exclude God from their lives, they will have to pay the price, whether they believe it or not. God *must* be our leader *at all costs.* It is the *ultimate heroic act* to let God use us as his soldiers. This means that all of our plans, thoughts, and desires belong to Him.

Men like Gideon, Jephthah, and Samson are known as heroes, physically. However, their personal lives were not heroic. To be a true hero, we must go into battle everyday in our *home, job, church, and society* to be examples to non-believers. Our weapons are the morals and the truth we receive from the teachings of Jesus Christ and from God's Word. We will lose the battle if our focus is on earthly treasures, instead of the treasures of heaven (Colossians 3:1-16).

Proverbs 13:6

When we live blamelessly, it helps us into living peaceful lives. We were placed into this world to obey God. The choices we make reflect our character. Every good choice leads to other opportunities for good, and the same goes for evil choices, only in the opposite pattern. Obedience toward God will lead to great blessings.

1 John 4:20-21

It is easy to say we love God. It is easy to go to church every week or whenever we feel like it. Anyone can do these things, but our true love for God reflects on how we treat the people around us. How? Because God created everybody else, just as He created you. We cannot love God if we refuse to love those who were created in His image (Matthew 5:43-48). When an individual mistreats you or disrespects you intentionally, they are not honoring God or showing any love towards Him.

HOW CAN I COMMIT MY LIFE TO GOD?

Proverbs 16:3

This scripture probably says it best. "Commit your actions to the Lord, and your plans will succeed." Some people "disguise" their work, by saying their work is being done for the Lord, when in reality they are doing it for themselves. Others give God temporary control of their plans, only to take control back the second things stop going their way. And others commit a task fully to the Lord, but put forth no effort themselves, and they'll wonder why they still fail.

God will help us with our tasks, however He will not complete it all for us. We must maintain this balance: trusting God as if everything depends on Him, while working as if everything depends on us. Think of a specific situation you are involved in now. Have you committed it to the Lord?

1 Peter 1:14-16

Peter's words are very wise. He said it straight out; that we should live our lives according to God's standards. But let's realize that none of us are perfect. After we commit our lives to Christ, we will sometimes fall short of living holy, and back to our old ways. However, Jesus gave us his Holy Spirit to help us obey and to give us the power to overcome sin. Peter's message is to be holy like our heavenly Father.

Holiness means being totally devoted and committed to God, seeking His ways and departing from sin. If we want to give up our life of sin, it helps to *be different* from others; not blending in with the crowd. Surround yourself with good company ".... for bad company corrupts good character" (1 Corinthians 15:33).

Our focus must be to live for God and put Him first above all things. Don't use the excuse that you can't help back-sliding into sin. Instead, rely on God's power to guide you and set you free from sin.

IF I AM A CHRISTIAN,
HOW AM I SUPPOSED TO LIVE?

John 17:18

Jesus asked God to use believers in the world. Because we were sent by God into the world, we should not try to escape from it. We shouldn't avoid all relationships with non-Christians either. We have been called to be salt and light (Matthew 5:13-16), and we are to do the work that God sent us to do.

1 Peter 8:9

Thomas, a disciple of Jesus, came to believe after he touched his resurrected body. Jesus said to him, "You believe because you have seen me. Blessed are those who believe without seeing me" (John 20:29). Peter heard those words and repeats it this way: "You love him even though you have never seen him."

That kind of faith brings us *salvation* and the *promise* of a life when pain and suffering *will end*. But what should we do until then? We must keep our faith high and continue to serve God at all costs. Even if that means to suffer through something, at least we know that *God is bigger than our problems,* and if we rely on His guidance, He will return with His reward.

A message from playwright, film-maker, and actor TYLER PERRY!

Tyler Perry is a celebrity whom I have incredible respect for. Why? Because he has endured some major challenges while growing up, and he didn't let any of those challenges stop him from being the successful man he is today. I've noticed that many of the events that took place in his life are elements he uses in his films. His films generally display Gospel themes and valuable messages to the audience, blended with a lot of humor, which I imagine takes a special kind of talent.

He is consistently posting blogs and messages on

his website --- TylerPerry.com, and I have subscribed to his site, so I can keep up with his postings/messages each time he adds one, via email.

One message I've read from his site was so powerful, amazing, and moving to me that I just had to share it with you! Enjoy!!!

Tyler Perry's message:

It's funny how a song, a taste, a scent, or something as simple as a change in weather can trigger a memory. Certain times of year make me think about when I was homeless. Especially the winter. I started thinking about this one lady in particular who helped me out during that time. She was a good soul who saw me in need and gave me money and food. She didn't have much but what she had she shared out of the kindness of her heart. I told her that when I got successful I would pay her back. She smiled and said, "You don't have to pay me anything. I just felt led to help you."

I couldn't stop thinking about her the other day so I

did some research and found her. Imagine her shock when I called her. She didn't even think that I remembered her. It's funny how something that was a small gesture to her was a huge blessing to me. As we went on talking, she reluctantly told me that she had just lost her job and was facing foreclosure. Of course, I did some things to help her out.

Why am I telling you this? I'm glad you asked. She gave to me out of the kindness of her heart. She gave to me from a pure place and expected nothing in return. The thing that brought tears to my eyes and blessed me so about this situation was this: this woman planted a seed in my life almost twenty years ago. But what she didn't know at the time was that the seed she planted would one day come back and bless her life just when she needed it most.

So what am I saying? I'm saying that if you are a giver of whatever you have... time, money, love, help, whatever it is... if you plant it in pureness it has got to come back to you. It may take a while but you will reap a harvest from that seed. Don't be weary in well-doing. It will come back to you. I know sometimes it may seem that all the good you do goes unnoticed by people, but if they don't notice, it doesn't matter. If they don't acknowledge your kindness, it does not matter. You know why? Because I promise you God sees it all and He is the only one that matters. And He is bound by His word, and that word says you will reap what you sow. So sow on, sow good seeds. They will grow and come back to you when you least expect it.

God bless you today.

by Tyler Perry on February 08, 2013

http://tylerperry.com/messages/it-may-take-time/

Can you see why I wanted to share this story with you? It reminds me of the Parable of the Great Samaritan (Luke 10:25-37). The lady in this story was like an angel. God sent her to do His work in the world, which was to help another individual created in His image.

What a great example of how we should treat one another isn't it? And look at what her blessing for Tyler Perry did for her in the end....

If you think you can't make a difference in someone's life, you have never been more wrong. What you put into this world is what you get back...even if it may take a while. The choice is yours.

> *Happiness doesn't result from what we get,*
> *but from what we give.*
> BEN CARSON

CHAPTER TEN

SEVEN REASONS NOT TO WORRY

"I've learned that no matter what happens or how bad it seems today, life does go on, and it will be a better tomorrow."
~ MAYA ANGELOU

When you worry, it can only *raise* your stress levels; (1) it can damage your health, (2) distract you from your goals, (3) negatively affect the way you treat others, and (4) reduce your faith in God.

Jesus teaches about Worrying in Matthew 6:25-34. And these are the seven reasons that further elaborate each passage on this topic:

Matthew Chapter 6

> **verse 25:** The same God who created life in you can be trusted with the details of your life.

verse 26:	Worrying about the future keeps you from enjoying the present day.
verse 27:	Worrying is clearly unhealthy.
verses 28-30:	God does not ignore those who rely on Him.
verses 31, 32:	Worrying shows a lack of faith in and understanding of God.
verse 33:	Worrying disrupts you from receiving the things you need from God.
verse 34:	Living one day at a time is less stressful and more helpful than worrying.

"Don't worry about anything; instead pray about everything. Tell God what you need and thank him for all he has done. Then you will experience God's peace, which will guard your hearts and minds as you live in Christ Jesus" (Philippians 4:6,7).

What harmful effects of worrying have you experienced? There is a difference between worrying and being concerned. Worrying is a waste of time and energy, but concerns can lead you to solving a problem you may have.

Dr. Frederick Price shares a method that God has shown him in his book, "The Truth About... Worry: How to Leave Your Cares Behind."

You get a piece of paper, or more than one if you need it, and write down every care you have that causes you to worry. When you are finished, take your list to the wastepaper basket, and say the following:

"Lord, you told me in the Bible to cast all my cares upon you. I cannot see you. I do not know where your hand is, so if I threw my cares at you, I am not sure if I would be throwing them in the right direction. So, as an act of faith, I am going to say that this piece of paper, with all of these things listed on it, represents all of my cares and all of my concerns. This wastepaper basket represents your hand. I cast these cares upon you, Father, in the name of Jesus."

When you finish saying that, ball up the paper, drop it in the wastepaper basket, and leave it there. Once you leave your list of worries there, you do not have them anymore. This method is based on the scripture, "Cast your cares upon Him, for He cares for you" 1 Peter 5:7. If you cast your cares on the Lord, the Lord has them and you do not, and you are free.

CHAPTER ELEVEN

THE TACTICS OF THE ENEMY

"Throughout life, people will make you mad, disrespect
you and treat you bad. Let God deal with the things they
do, cause hate in your heart will consume you too."
~ WILL SMITH

When you go to different places such as work, school, the mall, etc., always be aware of your surroundings. As Christians, we've got to understand that we are in a spiritual warfare and the enemy is trying to bombard your mind with pressure, overwhelming thoughts, and the wrong kind of people. We have to understand that we can no longer look in the mirror and see ourselves as civilians, we've got to see ourselves as soldiers.

We know who our enemy is. The Bible tells us our enemy is Satan and the Bible tells us what his agenda is. In John 10:10, it says he comes to do three things; steal, kill, and destroy.

So we know what his agenda is. My question is…. 'what is he trying to steal from you?' The answer is he's trying to steal your focus, your values, and your joy.

What is he trying to kill? He's trying to kill your reputation as a Christian, he's trying to kill you, and he's trying to kill your joy.

And what is he trying to destroy? He's trying to destroy your confidence in God's word and His goodness, so that you can put your focus on your problems instead of on God. He's trying to destroy your ability to tell right from wrong, and he's trying to destroy your dignity, so you'll feel like a failure; therefore, he wants to destroy your joy!

So as Christians, we need to be aware that when we go to our jobs, when we're going to school; when we're going out in public, the enemy is looking for an opportunity to gain access to cause you to lose your focus. We need to be soldiers.

I believe that every soldier deals with something called "Battle Fatigue". Fatigue means to be exhausted, weary, overworked, annoyed, or at the breaking point.

Another definition of fatigue is to crack under continual stress.

Have you ever been in a fight and you've gotten tired, whether it was natural or spiritual? What do you do when you've been dealing with something or someone for so long and you get tired? Sometimes you can't just let it go because if you do, it will take control of you. We have to fight; we have to make sure we stay on the defensive, and stand against what the devil is bringing against us.

I want to share "The Symptoms of Battle Fatigue" with you. I found it on a military website — http://armymedical.tpub.com, and I thought it was interesting because I found it to be very applicable to Satan's methods.

Symptoms of Battle Fatigue

1) "Thousand-yard-stare" - when you're staring off into space, and losing focus on what you're supposed to be paying attention to.

2) Hyperalertness - when your mind is being

bombarded with thoughts; when things are being thrown at your mind like grenades and land mines. They keep exploding in your head and it can cause you to lose sleep (see Insomnia, number 8).

3) Tension - when your fuse is so short, anything can tick you off.

4) Headaches

5) Depression (warning signs--silent withdrawal) - when you don't want to be around anyone or do anything.

6) Flight Tendency - when something doesn't go your way, so you just want to go AWOL. You want to give up and walk or run away.

7) Slow Reaction Time - being slow to respond to things because of a shell-shock you've been through.

8) Insomnia - not being able to sleep.

9) Isolation - disconnecting from your surroundings (the ones who care about you).

10) Inability to prioritize

We're understanding that Satan's agenda is to steal, kill, and destroy. Another thing we need to understand is that 2 Corinthians 2:11 says we are familiar with his evil schemes, so he will not outsmart us. Now let's put this all together. We know what his agenda is, we know what his evil schemes are, and we know what his methods are. Therefore, as believers, we've got to be on the watch *all the time*. The only way we're going to be able to deal with the pressures that are in the world is to constantly renew our minds and by hearing the word of God on a regular basis.

Matthew 4:1-11

When Jesus was fasting in the wilderness for forty days without food, he was tired, hungry, and worn out. Satan took this as an opportunity to tempt him into turning away from God. Satan had memorized Scripture to try to get Jesus to worship him, but Jesus was able to stay a few steps ahead because he also knew Scripture. Knowing Bible verses is an important tool in helping us resist the devil (Ephesians 6:10-17). With his knowledge and obedience, Jesus was able to resist all of the devil's temptations. As a result, the devil went away, and angels came and took care of Jesus. "So humble yourselves before God. Resist the devil, and he will flee from you" (James 4:7).

CHAPTER TWELVE

THE POWER OF PRAYER

*"Take the first step in faith. You don't have to see the
whole staircase, just take the first step."*
~ DR. MARTIN LUTHER KING, JR.

WHAT GOOD DOES PRAYER DO?

2 Chronicles 6:19-42

Solomon led his people in prayer and he asked God
to hear their prayers. Their prayers were concerning
crime, enemy attacks, war, and sin. God is concerned
with whatever we face. He wants us to come to Him in
prayer and rely on Him, instead of ourselves. It is
important to note that when you pray, God hears you.
How big or small your situations are does not matter to
Him; God wants you to talk to Him because He cares
about you.

Psalm 4:3

The godly are faithful children of God. They are devoted to obeying Him at all costs. David was confident about God hearing him when he called on him and that God would answer him.

If David can be this strong in confidence, so can we. Sometimes we may think that God will ignore us and our prayers because of our sinful behavior. But if we believe in our hearts that his Son, Jesus is Lord, God has forgiven us and He will listen to us. Our God is a forgiving God.

He hears and answers, according to his timetable. His answers may not always be what you expect, but that only means that the outcome will be the best. Our problems are just the beginning of us receiving some of God's power/blessings.

Jesus replied, "This kind can only be cast out by prayer" **(Mark 9:29)**

The disciples would often face difficulties that could be resolved only by prayer. Prayer is the battery that turns on our faith. Effective prayer needs the attitude of complete reliance, the action of asking, and the understanding that it must be done in God's will. Prayer demonstrates our dependence on God as we humbly invite him to guide us through faith and power.

You cannot substitute prayer for anything, especially when you're in a jam that only God can help you with. Also, remember that a key element in prayer is faith. "It is impossible to please God without faith" (Hebrews 11:6).

IF GOD SEES ALL AND KNOWS ALL, WHY PRAY?

Isaiah 38:1-5

Hezekiah is a great example of how we should behave when we have an emergency situation or when we are suffering in general. Hezekiah was extremely ill, and when the prophet Isaiah told him he was going to die, Hezekiah's reaction was to turn to God immediately. God's response to his prayer was to spare his life for another 15 years.

Like Hezekiah, when we're faced with difficult situations, we need to bring it to God. There is great power in genuine prayer. It may change the course of your life if you tell God what's on your heart; if you are honest with Him and yourself.

HOW SHOULD I PRAY?

Jonah 2:1-7

A thankful prayer is possibly one of the most effective prayers anyone can give to the Lord. We all have something to be thankful for, and we should express it towards God and his goodness.

Jonah's prayer was of thanksgiving. Although he was swallowed by a fish, Jonah was simply thankful that he hadn't drowned. While he was inside the fish, he prayed his thankful prayer, and God heard him. This provides a great example that God can hear us no matter where we are. No matter what we've done, our sins are never too great or too difficult for God.

Jonah said, "As my life was slipping away, I

remembered the Lord," (Jonah 2:7). Some of us may have the same mindset. When we are living happy lives, we may take God for granted, but when we're in desperate need, we call on him. God may possibly consider this kind of relationship to be unacceptable. We need to communicate with God during both our good and bad times. When things are going our way, we should bring our happiness to God and *thank* Him for his goodness.

If we keep this up, we will have a stronger relationship with God. Communication is the key to every healthy relationship, right? This applies with God too.

Mark 11:22-27

The kind of prayer that moves mountains is a prayer for the benefits of God's kingdom. Naturally, we would think it's impossible for a mountain to be moved into the sea, but Jesus used that illustration to show that with God everything is possible (Matthew 19:26). It takes more than just a positive mental attitude for God to answer your prayers. You must also (1) be a believer; (2) *forgive* those who have done wrong by you; (3) pray with unselfish motives; (4) consider what God may want.

Our best example, Jesus prayed, "Everything is possible for you... Yet I want your will to be done, not mine" (Mark 14:36). When Jesus prayed, he kept God's will for him in mind. It's okay for us to express our desires when we pray, but it is still important to request His will above ours. After all, God knows what's best.

Hebrews 4:16

Prayer is how we come to God. Prayer is the only way of keeping a strong relationship with God, so we are to come to Him boldly. Some people communicate with God in fear and/or doubt. Others may do it out of peer pressure from others. But when we come to God, we should be bold and happy to do so, because He is our King and our friend.

1 John 5:14-15

Although, we need to pray with confidence, we should never demand what we want from God. The motives behind our prayers should be about God's will for us, not our will for us. If our prayer requests pleases Him, He will listen to us and give us answers. Remember, God does not owe us *anything.* However, we owe it to Him to live each day as if it's our last, being completely devoted to Him. Tomorrow is *never* promised. We cannot be devoted to God without having a prayer life.

CHAPTER THIRTEEN

GETTING TO KNOW WHO GOD IS

*"I'm not perfect. And who knows how many times
I've fallen short. We all fall short. That's the amazing
thing about the grace of God."*
~ TIM TEBOW

Genesis 1:1

From reading the beginning of the Bible, we can understand that God is creative. He created the heavens and the earth and all people. He did not have to do it, nor did he need to do it, but God chose to do so because he loves us. His creation is an expression of his love for us, in fact God is love (1 John 4:8,16).

Since God chose to create us, we are obviously valuable to him. So if you are ever in a position where you may feel left out, unappreciated, beneath others, or just flat out worthless, just remember none of that can be true because God loves you. If any of that were true you wouldn't have been created by Him.

Sometimes, I myself, struggle to remember that God is in control of the world. Some of my troubles are totally out of my hands, however they are in His hands.

Numbers 14:17-20

In this section, you will find Moses pleading with God, asking Him to forgive his people. Several of God's characteristics are revealed in his plea. We can always count on God and his love; God forgives us when we come to him; God is merciful and willing to listen to us and answer us; and most importantly God is love. God is patient. Love is patient (1 Corinthians 13:4), so therefore God is love. He has not changed since Moses' time or the beginning of creation. We too can rely on God's love, patience, forgiveness, and mercy, just like Moses could.

Psalm 34:9-10

This is David's praise towards God's goodness. Even though, not all Christians have what they want, God knows what they need, and if we call upon Him in our need, He will answer us. Sometimes God answers us in unexpected ways.

Even though many Christians struggle with poverty and unbearable hardships, they still have enough spiritual strength to live for God. In this section of David's psalm, David was saying that God is all you really need. As long as you have God, you have enough.

If you feel that you don't have everything that you need, there may be a reason. God may allow you to go without certain things, so that you may depend on Him more. He would want to teach you that you need Him more than any of your personal desires. Why? Because God is our source for the things we truly need. What we need to do on our behalf is come close to Him. Then He will come close to us (James 4:8).

Psalm 36:5-8

God's power is stronger and more powerful than the forces of evil. This power is *love*, which expands to His faithfulness, His righteousness, and His just. His love is as strong as the heavens that He created; His faithfulness reaches beyond the clouds; His righteousness is as solid as the mighty mountains; His judgments are as full of wisdom as the oceans are with water. We do not need to fear evil people because God loves us, judges evil, and will take care of us throughout eternity. God's power is unlimited, as opposed to the limited power of evil.

Psalm 99:5

It is clear that God deserves our praises and our undivided attention to Him, simply because He is *holy*. This is frightening for sinners because all of their evil desires are exposed by the light of God's holiness. For believers, God's holiness gives comfort because we worship him. Our worship to God lifts us away from sin and closer to Him. As we believe in Him and humble ourselves before Him, we are made holy and set apart from sin.

John 14:5-6

Now this is one of the most important scriptures in the Word. How can we know the way to God? It is through Jesus Christ, *the only way*. Jesus is the way because he is God's Son and God sent Him to die on the cross for our sins. Why? Because God loves us (John 3:16). By uniting our lives with Jesus, we are united with God.

2 Thessalonians 2:10-12

This provides a good understanding of God's nature. We understand that God is good (Psalm 11:7); God created a good world that fell because of humanity's sin (Romans 5:12); One day, God will re-create the world and it will be good again (Revelation 21:1); God is stronger than evil (Matthew 13:41-43); God allows evil, however He did not create it. He uses everything, both good and evil, for His good purposes (Genesis 50:20; Romans 8:28).

So you see, we as mere people do not need to understand every detail of how our God works. We can still have perfect confidence in his power over evil, and just *trust* that He will continue to be good to us.

CHAPTER FOURTEEN

THE GOODNESS OF JESUS/FOCUS ON GRATITUDE

"My mother was one of the most spiritual people I knew but she didn't raise me in the church, so I came to my Christian faith later in life and it was because the precepts of Jesus Christ spoke to me in terms of the kind of life that I would want to lead."
~ BARACK OBAMA

WHAT KIND OF PEOPLE DID JESUS ASSOCIATE WITH?

Jesus came to know many different types of people. He reached out to all of them, regardless of how rich or poor, great or unknown, young or old, sinner or saint; He loves us all equally. Here is a list of the people Jesus associated with and how different they were from one another.

A despised tax collector	(Matthew 9:9)
An insane hermit	(Mark 5:1-15)
The Roman governor	(Mark 15:1-15)
A young boy	(Mark 9:17-27)
A young girl	(Mark 5:35-43)
A homemaker	(Luke 10:38-42)
A criminal	(Luke 23:40-43)
Fishermen	(Matthew 4:18-20)
A king	(Luke 23:7-11)
A poor widow	(Luke 7:11-17)
A Roman captain	(Luke 7:1-10)
A group of children	(Mark 10:13-16)
An adulterous woman	(John 8:1-11)
A sick woman	(Mark 5:25-34)
A rich man	(Mark 10:17-23)
A blind beggar	(Mark 10:46)
A group of women	(Luke 8:2,3)
The high priest	(Matthew 26:62-68)
An angry mob of soldiers and guard	(John 18:3-9)
An outcast with leprosy	(Luke 17:11-19)
A traitor	(John 13:1-3, 27)

A helpless and paralyzed man   (Mark 2:1-12)

A woman from a foreign land   (Mark 7:25-30)

An enemy who hated him   (Acts 9:1-9)

EXPECT THE UNEXPECTED

Jesus did the unexpected wherever he went. He exceeded people's expectations to show that no matter what we may want or expect, Jesus knows what's best!

WHAT WAS EXPECTED   **WHAT JESUS DID**

A man looked for healing.   Jesus also forgave his sins.

Mark 2:1-12

The disciples were expecting   They found the Savior
an ordinary day of fishing.

Luke 5:1-11

A widow was resigned to   Jesus restored her son
bury her dead son.   to life.

Luke 7:11-17

| The religious leaders wanted a miracle. | Jesus offered them the Creator of miracles. |

Matthew 12:38-45

| A woman who wanted to be healed touched Jesus. | Jesus helped her see it was her faith that healed her. |

Mark 5:25-34

| The disciples thought the crowd should be sent home because there was no food. | Jesus used a small meal to feed the thousands, and there were leftovers! |

John 6:1-15

| The disciples wanted to eat the Passover meal with Jesus, their Master. | Jesus washed their feet, showing that he was also their servant. |

John 13:1-20

| The religious leaders wanted Jesus killed and got their wish. | But Jesus rose from the dead! |

John 20:1-29

WHAT DID JESUS DO FOR US?

Mark 15:31

When Jesus was on that cross, he could have saved himself without a doubt. He could have chosen not to take the pain and humiliation. He could have also killed those who mocked and hurt him. But *he suffered* through it all because of his love for us, even his enemies. Jesus made the best out of a horrible, painful situation.

He used his suffering to express his love for all of humanity and for God. We too can *use our suffering* for God and giving back to Jesus by staying devoted to him. Just think, none of us would even be here to live our lives or do anything if Jesus hadn't suffered the way he did *for us*. This is *the most important event in history* to keep in mind. Never take it for granted!

Colossians 1:12-14

Here are five benefits God has given all believers through Jesus: (1) He enabled us to share in his inheritance; (2) He rescued us from the kingdom of darkness and made us his children; (3) He brought us into his eternal kingdom; (4) He purchased our freedom and judgment with his blood; and (5) He forgave all our sins.

Focus less on your problems and thank God for the precious gifts you have received through Jesus Christ. They are the *greatest gifts* anyone could ever receive. Whether we realize it or not, we have a lot to be thankful for, even in the midst of our distress. When you take things for granted, the things you are granted get taken. Always be thankful.

*** I would like to challenge you to *focus on gratitude.* Spend at least five minutes per day alone with God. Don't ask for anything during those five minutes, just thank Him for all He's done for you. Thank Him for what you have. Never convince yourself that you can never find the time to do this, because a thought like this comes from the enemy. You can spend time with God, while you are driving somewhere everyday. Just praying and talking to Him, as you are paying attention to your driving or while you're at a red light. You can even spare some time on your lunch breaks to be alone with God. I challenge you to practice spending time with God in silence, wait patiently for God to answer your prayers, and see what blessings come your way.***

REFERENCE

Notes taken from the Life Application Study Bible
(New Living Translation).

Symptoms of Battle Fatigue
http://armymedical.tpub.com/MD0549/MD05490023.htm

Asperger Syndrome
http://en.wikipedia.org/wiki/Asperger_syndrome
http://www.ninds.nih.gov/disorders/asperger/detail_asperger.htm
https://www.autismspeaks.org/what-autism/asperger-syndrome
http://aspennj.org/what-is-asperger-syndrome

"Set your affection on things above, not on things on the earth." – Colossians 3:2 (KJV)

"For our present troubles are small and won't last very long. Yet they produce for us a glory that vastly outweighs them and will last forever! So we don't look at the troubles we can see now; rather, we fix our gaze on things that cannot be seen. For the things we see now will soon be gone, but the things we cannot see will last forever." – 2 Corinthians 4:17-18 (NLT)

Derek White

www.ingramcontent.com/pod-product-compliance
Lightning Source LLC
Chambersburg PA
CBHW060418050426
42449CB00009B/2024